I0150442

School Cents...

The Energy Behavior

Management Guide

By Sue Pierce

Energy Consultant

Copyright © 2011 by Sue Pierce

All rights reserved. No parts of this book may be used or reproduced in any manner whatsoever without written permission except in the case of brief quotations embodied in critical articles and review.

Printed in the United States of America

For more information and to find out about special discounts for bulk purchases, please contact sue@energyplanning.org

Cataloging-in-Publication Data is on file with the Library of Congress

ISBN – 13: 978-0-9833265-0-2

ISBN – 10:   0-9833265-0-2

All rights reserved.

Edited by Wendy VanHatten, Vacaville, California
Cover and Interior Layout by The Printed Page, Phoenix, Arizona
Photograph by Michael Corbin, Sioux City, Iowa

This book is printed on recycled paper.

Table of Contents

Introduction   Page i

Chapter One   Preparing Your Energy Strategy   Page 1

Chapter Two   Creating Energy Policy and Standards   Page 17

Chapter Three   Energy Benchmarks and Data Management   Page 26

Chapter Four   The Energy Teams   Page 36

Appendix A   Resources   Page 47

Appendix B   Sample Energy Policy Statements   Page 48

Appendix C   Sample Energy Standards   Page 50

Appendix D   Energy Team Materials   Page 59

About the Author   Page 71

Introduction

"The difference between what we do and what we are capable of doing would suffice to solve most of the world's problems." - Mahatma Gandhi

Sometimes we don't know what is possible until someone shows us.

For years, the 4-minute mile was considered not merely unreachable but, according to physiologists of the time, dangerous to the health of any athlete who attempted to reach it.

For many years it was widely believed to be impossible for a human to run a mile (1609 meters) in under four minutes. In fact, for many years, it was believed that the four minute mile was a physical barrier that no man could break without causing significant damage to the runner's health. The achievement of a four minute mile seemed beyond human possibility... like climbing Mount Everest or walking on the moon... And yet, on May 6, 1954, during an athletic meeting between the British AAA and Oxford University Roger Bannister crossed the finish line with a time of 3 minutes, 59.4 seconds, and broke through the "four minute mile" psychological barrier. Within three years, 16 other runners also cracked the four minute mile. So what happened to the physical barrier that prevented humans from running the four minute mile? Was there a sudden leap in human evolution?

No.

It was the change in thinking that made the difference. Bannister had shown that breaking the four minute mile was possible. Others now saw that it was possible and then 16 runners went on to do the same.

And so it is in my work. Saving energy in schools through behavior is all about believing that it is possible and that it can be done. Many of the barriers that hold us back today exist only in our minds.

When I first started working with school districts on saving energy, many elected officials and superintendents were skeptical. "We wish you well, but I don't think simple behavior changes will do much." "You think we can reduce energy use by 10% through behavior changes? No way!"

Twelve months later that District had reduced energy use by 15% across approximately 3,000,000 square feet of building space. Twenty four months later the program had reduced consumption by 26% for an avoided electric energy cost of over $2,000,000. And yes, now they are believers as are many other school districts I work with!

At a time when money is desperately needed in the classroom, it breaks my heart to see schools ignoring the money that could be saved by changing simple ways of behaving in the buildings. *School Cents...The Energy Behavior Management Guide* is a step by step guide on how to save energy through behavior modification. I have taken the process I have used over and over with great success and documented it here for other school districts to use.

This Guidebook will provide you with the basic tools you need to implement an energy behavior management program in-house with District staff and to keep the energy savings in the District.

Each chapter in the book addresses critical components of the program in logical order. Start at the beginning. Many will be tempted to skip around and pick and choose the chapter(s) they like ignoring those they do not like. Unfortunately, each chapter in this guidebook addresses an essential component of the program. Complete the exercises and tasks outlined in Chapter One before moving on to Chapter Two and so on. In this way, you will set yourself up for success.

There is power in the process! We are changing school cultures and helping people believe that their actions taken collectively can make a big difference. Time to start this exciting journey!

Sue Pierce
Energy Consultant
Pierce and Associates Company

Chapter One - Preparing Your Energy Strategy

"Spectacular achievement is always preceded by spectacular preparation." – Robert H. Schuller

As a school official, you probably know the annual energy bill to run America's primary and secondary schools is a staggering $6 billion — more than is spent on textbooks and computers combined. What you may not know is that the least efficient schools use three times more energy than the best energy performers and that the top energy performing schools cost $.40 per square foot less to operate than the average performers. These statistics are from ENERGY STAR™, a program of the United States Environmental Protection Agency.

Schools can play a valuable role in teaching students about becoming energy efficient and in leading their communities to become more efficient, too. In the process, you positively impact the environment, teach social responsibility, and help the school district save money on energy bills.

In this chapter, you will learn the key elements of an energy strategy; discuss critical issues impacting an Energy Behavior Management Program in your school; and lay the ground work for creating an energy team and plan for your school.

Prepare to Plan: Visioning, Mission, and Goals

The first step in creating an energy strategy is to create a vision, a mission statement, and strategic goals for your school community. It is important to know what you are all working to accomplish. Let's begin by defining some key terms we will be using and by providing some examples of each:

What is "visioning"?

Visioning is a mental process in which images of the desired future (goals, objectives, out-comes) are made intensely real and compelling. The vision motivates stakeholders to take action. A successful Energy Behavior Management Program begins with a compelling vision articulated by the superintendent and supported by the school board. The vision is communicated throughout the organization to all stakeholders. There is no doubt in anyone's mind regarding the district's support for the energy program. The vision is discussed frequently at public and district meetings so that it is clearly kept in the forefront. As the energy program is implemented, the vision reaches out to all staff, students, parents, and community members. It is much like a pebble thrown into water. As the compelling vision is communicated, it has a ripple effect that eventually encompasses the entire community and in this way culture is transformed.

Features of an effective vision statement include:

- Clarity and lack of ambiguity
- Vivid and clear picture
- Description of a bright future
- Memorable and engaging wording
- Realistic aspirations
- Alignment with organizational values and culture

Many examples of vision statements can be found on the Internet. I have included a few here for your review. However, I encourage you to do your own research and create a vision statement that best fits your school/district.

Sample Energy/Sustainability Vision Statements

1. Lane Community College Sustainability Vision

   Imagine a Lane Community College where:

   - ongoing operations result in a minimal negative impact on our natural environment.
   - we are actively engaged in creating ways to positively impact our environment.
   - continuous learning takes place about our impact on the environment, as a college and as individuals.
   - sustainability is a way of thinking about everything we do; every staff member takes personal responsibility for creating and using sustainable practices and principles in our daily work.
   - we integrate sustainability into our relationships and the social fabric of the college.

2. Charter Films Sustainability Vision Statement

   Charter Films will strive to reduce the impact our internal operations have on the environment through sustainable practices and source reduction initiatives. In addition, we will seek to provide our customers with solutions designed to help them produce products that are inherently more sustainable.

3. Emory University Sustainability Vision Statement

   Sustainability is defined as meeting the needs of the present generation without compromising the needs of future generations. As part of its commitment to positive transformation in the world, Emory has identified sustainability as a top priority of the university included in Emory's Strategic Plan. Emory's vision calls on the Office of Sustainability Initiatives to help restore our global ecosystem, foster healthy living, and reduce the University's impact on the local environment. Progress will be assessed using the environmental, economic, and social "triple bottom line" of sustainability. When applying the triple bottom line of sustainability, the decisions and choices made by Emory must pass a new set of filters: What is the social impact of this decision? The environmental impact? The economic impact? What will be the local impact? The global impact? The impact to future generations?

4. Lethbridge Primary School Sustainability Vision Statement

   We will to engage students, staff, and the community in our quest to develop a sustainable school environment.

Exercise #1 – Write Your Vision

Write a vision for your Energy Behavior Management Program.

_____

_____

_____

_____

_____

_____

_____

_____

_____

_____

_____

_____

What is a "mission statement"?

The Energy Behavior Management Program requires a mission statement. The mission statement serves as a filter to separate what is important from what is not important. It clearly identifies the stakeholders of the school; the general actions that will be taken; the direction to be pursued. A mission is something to be accomplished whereas a vision is something to be pursued for that accomplishment. Many examples can be found on the Internet. I have included a few here for your review. Once again, create the mission statement that best states your intentions.

Sample Energy/Sustainability Mission Statements

1. The mission of the PVUSD Energy Conservation Committee is to promote energy conservation awareness by providing strategies that reduce utility costs and empower students and staff to take ownership in reducing carbon emissions and saving valuable district funds, while modeling energy conservation habits for future generations.

2. Wisconsin Energy Conservation Corporation - we champion innovative energy initiatives that deliver short-term and long-term economic and environmental benefits to consumers, businesses, and policy makers.

3. NEED Mission Statement – The mission of the NEED Project is to promote an energy conscious and educated society by creating effective networks of students, educators, business, government, and community leaders to design and deliver objective, multi-sided energy education programs.

Exercise #2 – Write Your Mission Statement

Write a mission statement for your Energy Behavior Management Program.

_____

_____

_____

_____

What are" strategic goals"?

The third key term to understand is strategic goals. The Oxford Dictionary defines "goal" as follows: "Point marking end of race; object of effort or ambition; destination." Many management consultants say that a goal is a specific, measurable occurrence, object, or accomplishment that the organization would like to achieve or obtain in the future. The Energy Behavior Management Program should have both long-term goal(s) and short-term goal(s). An example of a long-term goal could be "we will reduce our electric energy usage by 40% over the next five years." An example of a shorter term goal could be "we will reduce our electric energy usage by 10% in fiscal year 2011 – 2012."

A tool often used to help organizations set goals is the acronym SMART. Use of the SMART goal setting technique helps you avoid the five classic goal-setting mistakes.

A SMART Goal is:

Specific
Measurable
Achievable
Relevant
Time Specific

Exercise #3 – Write Long Term Goals

Write the long term strategic goals for your Energy Behavior Management Program.

_____

_____

_____

_____

_____

_____

Exercise #4 – Write Short Term Goals

Write the short term strategic goals for your Energy Behavior Management Program. Follow the SMART Rules.

_____

_____

_____

_____

_____

_____

_____

Defining Culture – Identifying Values

A culture is a shared, learned, symbolic system of values, beliefs, and attitudes that shapes and influences perception and behavior. A culture that embraces energy conservation is one where the stakeholders agree that saving energy is a good thing. They agree that by saving energy they can improve the environment and be more sustainable. They agree that by saving energy they as a school community can teach important values regarding preserving scarce resources and in the process also model leadership and responsibility. In addition, they realize that as a school community they can save money by reducing the use of electricity, natural gas, water, and solid waste. Many schools are facing tough economic times and saving energy can help the budget. A culture of energy conservation in a school contributes to the school community in many ways.

What values support an Energy Behavior Management Program? An organization makes decisions about policy, people, and operations from a specific set of values. The values are like a pair of colored glasses that influence our perspective. An organization that values people will make policies with their well- being in mind. Such an organization may place a high value on medical insurance programs, child-care issues, and assuring staff can take vacations. An Energy Behavior Management Program is best supported by shared values that include a willingness to work together as a team, a positive "can do" attitude, and a passion to conserve scarce natural resources. When these values are in place, the Energy Behavior Management Program is supported. If these values are not in place, leadership is needed to bring them into the organization.

Exercise #5 – Our Culture and Values

List five values you share as a school community? Circle the values that support energy conservation.

1. _____
2. _____
3. _____
4. _____
5. _____

Program Leadership

What types of leadership are needed to create a successful Energy Behavior Management Program? Leaders are critical to the success of an Energy Behavior Management Program. In its essence, leadership in an organization involves (1) establishing a clear vision, (2) sharing (communicating) that vision with others so they will follow willingly, (3) providing the information, knowledge, and methods to realize that vision, and (4) coordinating and balancing the conflicting interests of all members or stakeholders. In a school, the principal and administrators with the support of a carefully selected planning team usually work together to identify the vision and mission and communicate it to stakeholders. However, all staff and students in the school community have a critical leadership role to plan in the program. Every action a student takes to conserve energy or remind others to conserve energy is leadership. Each time the principal brings up the subject of energy conservation in a newsletter or at a meeting, he is exhibiting leadership. Teachers who discuss energy conservation in the classroom and use it as a teaching lesson are exhibiting leadership. Facility staff who monitor building equipment and grounds to make sure all is functioning properly and efficiently are showing leadership. The Energy Behavior Management Program is best supported when everyone on the school campus realizes that they have a leadership role to play in saving energy.

A change in culture occurs when all stakeholders identify with the vision and take some responsibility for bringing it about. Administrators are change agents. As the most visible leaders in the organization everyone is watching what they do. In a school, staff, students, and parents respond to the direction set by the principal. If the principal takes action to turn off lights, use day-lighting whenever possible, and maintain district standards for temperature set-points in his office, the school community understands he is committed to the vision. They will follow this example. Building staff are change agents. Students watch to see what they are willing to do to save energy. Do teachers implement energy education into the curriculum? Do teachers encourage energy fairs and Earth Day events? Do teachers turn off lights, use day-lighting whenever possible, and maintain district standards for temperature set-points in the classroom? Office and facility staff are very visible to the entire school community. They also are most aware of what is going on in the building. They can play a key role in supporting the energy program. Students are watching and will follow their example. Students are change agents. Students can be the greatest cheerleaders for an energy program. When staff forget to take action, students are great at reminding them. Students love to participate in a wide variety of energy experiments and activities. They are a vital part of any building energy team.

Exercise #6 – Identify Stakeholders Who Should Be Involved in the Energy Program

Identify stakeholders who should be a part of the energy program at your school. What role should they play? What are some activities where they would be involved?

STAKEHOLDER	THEIR ROLE	POSSIBLE ACTIVITIES

Empowerment and Long-term Success

What is empowerment? Is it more effective in the creation of a culture of energy conservation? First of all, let's define the term "empowerment". As used here empowerment means the management practice of sharing information, rewards, and power with employees so they can take initiative and make decisions to solve problems and to improve service and performance. As all stakeholders are a part of the school campus culture, only through their buy-in and participation can this culture be changed for the long-term. Sharing information is critical so they can be informed. Sharing decision-making gives employees and students ownership of the program. These are their ideas and the success and/or failure of the program will be their responsibility. Shared rewards are the pay-off for their hard work and commitment to the program.

Successes are to be celebrated! The concept of empowerment gives staff and students the skills, resources, authority, opportunity, and motivation to fully engage in the energy program. In addition, through empowerment they are held responsible and accountable for the outcomes of their actions. Empowerment supports positive attitudes.

Positive attitudes best support the Energy Behavior Management Program. Positive attitudes are modeled by the principal first and this example spreads to staff and students. The Energy Behavior Management Program can be a learning tool for the school community. Make it fun for everyone and take time to celebrate and publicly acknowledge successes. Take positive actions in support of energy conservation and positive feelings and attitudes are sure to follow.

Communication – complete and thorough - is one component of empowerment. It is important that everyone in the school community be informed over and over again about the energy program. As the best marketers say, an individual must be exposed to a message seven times before they internalize it. The principal can explain the program to staff and students before the energy audit and energy team are created, thus sharing the district vision and goals. Building announcements, staff meetings, the school web site, and the school newsletter are great ways to communicate with all stakeholders. After the building energy audit is complete and the energy team is in place, individual team members can share the responsibility of communicating with certain stakeholders. As each energy goal is reached, the entire district and community will welcome hearing about the schools successes. School board meetings, principal meetings, the district web site, the district newsletter, and press releases are some ways to get the word out to the public.

Exercise #7 – Communication

What communication tools and methods could be used in your school to keep everyone informed about the Energy Behavior Management Program?

_____

_____

_____

_____

_____

_____

_____

_____

_____

Who Are Your Energy Cheerleaders?

A challenge most schools face is how to get everyone fully engaged in the Energy Behavior Management Program. The best way is to identify an energy cheerleader(s) or advocate(s). These cheerleaders are people who are passionate about the environment, energy conservation, and/or sustainability. They also have credibility with other school stakeholders. The energy conservation advocates could be students, staff, parents, and/or members of the community who are active with the school. These advocates become the core energy team members and work with the principal to expand the committee. Their leadership, passion, and persistence in communicating the vision to all stakeholders will attract others to the cause.

Cultures change over time and not overnight. It can take time to identify Energy Behavior Management Program advocates especially if the school has not engaged in any energy or sustainability initiatives in the past. It often takes numerous communications over time to get a person's attention. Getting everyone in a school community (or at least most) on board is a huge task. Initially, the results are hard to quantify. Significant results occur over time. For all of these reasons, persistence is critical to the Energy Behavior Management Program and its viability in the long term.

Exercise #8 – Our Energy Cheerleaders

Do you have energy cheerleaders at your school? Write down some characteristics they display which supports your answer.

_____

_____

_____

_____

_____

_____

_____

_____

_____

Preparing Your Energy Strategy

Key Points to Remember

Successful Energy Behavior Management Program is well thought out and well planned.

Many school districts skip the first step, creating an energy strategy, and by so doing compromise the ultimate success of the program.

An energy strategy involves creating the vision, mission, and goals.

Everyone in the school community has a role to play in the Energy Behavior Management Program.

Find the energy cheerleaders to advocate for your cause and help you implement the program.

Empowerment of staff and students within the school creates buy-in and long term savings eventually leading to a cultural change.

NOTES

Chapter Two – Creating Energy Policy and Standards

"Would you tell me, please, which way I ought to go from here?" "That depends a good deal on where you want to get to," said the Cat. "I don't much care where" said Alice. "Then it doesn't matter which way you go," said the Cat" - Alice's Adventures in Wonderland by Lewis Carroll

The American Association of School Administrators states that the typical school district spends $400,000 each year on utility bills; some generate costs as high as $20 million per year. The U.S. Department of Energy (DOE) estimates that many districts could save 25 percent of that money through energy behavior management programs, better building design, widely available energy technologies, renewable energy use, and improvements to operations and maintenance.

Nationally, the estimated savings could pay for 40 million new textbooks, 30,000 new teachers or 1.5 million new computers every year. To support quality energy programs, the Department of Energy recommends that schools adopt smart energy policies and the standards (procedures) that detail how to implement the policy.

Schools that adopt and implement smart energy policies in their buildings, schools, buses, and classrooms save money but also receive many other benefits:

- Classrooms are more conducive to learning, with better lighting, better temperature control, air quality, and less outside noise.
- Students learn about energy conservation and how they can contribute to the environment.
- Buses emit fewer dangerous pollutants, particularly into areas where children learn and play.
- Schools spend less time and ultimately fewer resources maintaining and operating buildings and buses.
- The community appreciates the district's wise use of taxpayers' money.

In this chapter, you will learn the do's and don'ts related to creating and implementing an energy conservation policy; the importance of a separate standards (procedures) document; and what resources are available to support you in creating your own policy and standards statements.

Energy Conservation Policy

What is an energy conservation policy? An energy conservation policy is a statement(s) containing the principles, rules, and guidelines formulated by administration and adopted by the school board to reach its long-term energy goals and to achieve its energy mission and vision. The policy is designed to influence and determine all major decisions and actions related to the Energy Behavior Management Program.

Some school administrators object to creating policies thinking the policy may in some way restrict their decision-making ability and limit their flexibility. Since policy making is a function of the elected school board, a policy statement usually must go through a public review process including several readings before the board and prior to final adoption. It is cumbersome to create and difficult to change. Policies by their nature are broader statements that address the philosophical issues and as such are not changed frequently.

The advantages of having an energy conservation policy statement far outweigh the disadvantages especially if the policy is written correctly. The policy statement provides direction, focus, and credibility to the Energy Behavior Management Program. During implementation of the energy program, the policy statement adopted by the board puts all district staff on notice that this is the direction we will pursue. It gives the energy team authority to carry out their mission sometimes in the face of objections. The policy aligns all district departments so the independent actions of each works together to achieve the energy vision. For example, after the district installs new energy efficient lighting in a school, purchasing will need to shift buying habits and carry the new replacement products. The energy policy supports this alignment as well as consistent decision-making to bring about a universal objective. The policy further influences planning and budgeting decisions.

Policy implementation can be challenging. How does the district go about communicating policy changes to staff and obtaining district-wide buy-in? Is the policy adopted and thereafter put in a book on the shelf or sent off into the Internet never to be seen again? The success of the energy program will require the energy policy be a living and vibrant statement of how the district will conduct its business from this point forward. It will be the superintendent and administrators' responsibility to see that all staff members are informed. Principal, administrator, staff, and departmental meetings are opportunities to spread the word, and not just one time. Staff members need to hear the message regularly or an update regarding it. The policy can be put on the district web site, in newsletters, and sent out to the community through press releases. It should be revisited annually and reaffirmed or modified. **Sample Energy/Sustainability Policy Statements – See Appendix B**

Exercise #9 –Energy Conservation Policy

Write an energy conservation policy for your school district. Use the samples as a guide.

_____

_____

_____

_____

_____

_____

_____

_____

_____

_____

_____

_____

_____

_____

_____

Energy Conservation Standards

Standards are the specific methods employed to express policies in action in day-to-day operations of the organization. You may also hear them referred to as procedures. The terms as used here mean the same thing. Together, policies and standards ensure that a point of view held by the governing body of an organization is translated into steps that result in an outcome compatible with that view.

Although many school districts combine the energy conservation policy and standards into one document approved by the school board, I recommend keeping them separate. In a school district, policy is established through official board action and is seldom changed whereas standards are properly defined as a function of management meaning that the superintendent can approve them. By not mixing a policy document with a management document, the district has greater flexibility to make changes in the latter. Standards, by their nature, need to be altered, added to or deleted from periodically. An example may best illustrate this. One school district created temperature set points in their energy standards, which is a good thing to do. However, the summer set-point for unoccupied buildings was too high and floor tile started to curl in the heat. It was critical to adjust the set-point quickly and they did. Their standards were in a separate document from the policy statement, approval to modify was quickly obtained, and the change made without taking it to the school board. It is always best to separate policy functions from management functions whenever possible.

Energy conservation standards are easy to create. There are many templates available on the Internet. A few samples are included in Appendix C at the end of this document. Initially, the district must decide which types of energy they want to include in their conservation program. Will the program be limited to electricity and natural gas or will it include water conservation, too? What about recycling efforts to reduce the amount of waste sent to the landfill by the school? How about fuel used by district buses? Once the district decides on a scope for its program, look at some templates and samples specific to your climate and write away.

The difficult part is standards implementation. How do you inform, educate, and get all staff on-board? Some staff will view the standards as restrictive as well as limiting their flexibility to do their job. Some staff is resistant to change and want to do things as they always have. District administrators and the energy cheerleaders in the buildings must pave the way initially until the others are willing to buy-in. A valuable tool to use is the energy policy as few staff will argue with a directive from the board. In time, as results occur and are communicated, support for the program will grow.

Standards move the district towards the "right" actions; actions that support the energy conservation policy and help the district achieve its energy goals. The standards align all departments and assure that building management relative to energy conservation is consistent across all campuses. In this way, energy savings will be maximized and the program will endure. **Sample Energy/Sustainability Standards – See Appendix C**

Exercise #10 –Energy Conservation Standards

List 10 energy conservation standards that should be used to manage buildings in your district. Use the samples as a guide.

_____

_____

_____

_____

_____

_____

_____

_____

Creating Energy Policy and Standards

Key Points to Remember

An energy policy formulated by administration and adopted by the school board influences and guides all major decisions and actions related to the energy conservation policy.

The advantages of having an energy policy far outweigh the disadvantages of having one.

Energy standards are specific methods employed to express policies in day to day action.

Avoid the pitfall of combining energy policy and standards in one document (policy is a function of governance and standards are management functions).

Do not recreate the wheel – sample policy and standards documents can be found on the Internet and customized to meet your needs.

NOTES

Chapter Three – Benchmarks and Data Management

"Quality is never an accident; it is always the result of high intention, sincere effort, intelligent direction and skillful execution; it represents the wise choice of many alternatives." – William A. Foster

Data is the fuel that drives the Energy Behavior Management Program. Data analysis allows us to determine where we are today in terms of energy use in each of our buildings, thus creating a baseline for future comparison. Data supports decision-making regarding where and how to spend resources to improve energy performance. Data allows us to track our daily, weekly or monthly progress toward our goals. Data when put into easily understandable reports, supports competition among the schools participating in the Energy Behavior Management Program.

What is benchmarking?

The term benchmarking was first used by cobblers to measure people's feet for shoes. They would place someone's foot on a "bench" and mark it out to make the pattern for the shoes. Benchmarking is most used to measure performance using a specific indicator (cost per unit of measure, productivity per unit of measure, cycle time of x per unit of measure or defects per unit of measure) resulting in a metric of performance that is then compared to others. In relation to the energy program, benchmarking is the process of comparing the energy usage and performance of your schools to other schools throughout the country.

What is a baseline?

Baseline and benchmark are similar but distinct activities. A baseline is your building energy performance over a specific period of time. It serves as a point of comparison for future reference.

What is ENERGY STAR™ Portfolio Manager?

Portfolio Manager is a free interactive energy management tool that allows you to track and assess energy and water consumption across your entire portfolio of buildings in a secure online environment. Portfolio Manager can help you identify under-performing buildings, verify efficiency improvements, and receive EPA recognition for superior energy performance. ENERGY STAR™ is a recognized name throughout the country and a great tool for school districts to use.

How Does ENERGY STAR™ Portfolio Manager Work?

ENERGY STAR™ provides extensive information on their web site regarding how to set up an account in Portfolio Manager and how to begin the process of benchmarking buildings. General information detailed here was taken from the ENERGY STAR™ web site. For more in depth discussions of these concepts go to www.energystar.gov. You will need to log in to Portfolio Manager, create an account, and enter specific information about each of your buildings. A data checklist showing information you will need is shown below. After all data and information for a building has been properly entered, the building will be given an ENERGY STAR™ rating or benchmark.

The national energy performance rating is a type of external benchmark that helps energy managers assess how efficiently their buildings use energy, relative to similar buildings nationwide. The rating system's 1–100 scale allows everyone to quickly understand how a building is performing — a rating of 50 indicates average energy performance, while a rating of 75 or better indicates top performance.

The Environmental Protection Agency (EPA), in conjunction with stakeholders, developed the energy rating as a screening tool; it does not by itself explain why a building performs a certain way, or how to change the building's performance. It does, however, help organizations assess performance and identify those buildings that offer the best opportunities for improvement and recognition.

How is the rating calculated?

Based on the information you entered about your building, such as its size, location, number of occupants, number of PCs, etc., the rating system estimates how much energy the building would use if it were the best performing, the worst performing, and every level in between. The system then compares the actual energy data you entered to the estimate to determine where your building ranks relative to its peers.

All of the calculations are based on source energy. The use of source energy is the most equitable way to compare building energy performance and also correlates best with environmental impact and energy cost.

Specific data analysis, and statistical information about the rating methodology can be found in the ENERGY STAR™ document Model Technical Descriptions. This document is available at www.energystar.gov.

K-12 School Data Checklist:

- The building street address
- The month/year built & first occupied
- Contact information
- Most recent 12 consecutive months of utility bills for each meter and fuel type(s) used in the building. If you don't have this information readily available, contact your utility provider(s) as most will be able to easily supply this historical information.
- Gross floor area (SF)
- # of personal computers
- # of walk-in refrigeration/freezer units
- High school - yes or no
- Open weekends – yes or no
- On-site cooking – yes or no
- Percent of floor area that is cooled in 10% increments (10%, 20%, 30%, etc.)
- Percent of floor area that is heated in 10% increments (10%, 20%, 30%, etc.)
- Months of use (optional data)
- School District (optional data)

What Can I Do With Portfolio Manager?

Portfolio Manager supports the school district in managing energy and water consumption for all buildings. It allows you to rate building energy performance to determine which buildings are more or less energy efficient. This information can help you make decisions related to how capital and maintenance dollars will be spent and assist in facility planning and budgeting processes. Through Portfolio Manager you can estimate your carbon footprint today and track changes over time. The school district is able to gain various EPA recognitions which can demonstrate to the community your commitment to energy conservation and the wise use of tax dollars. ENERGY STAR™ has many tools available to help you both in energy efficient design, construction, and management of school facilities and all of these resources are free. ENERGY STAR™ Portfolio Manager is an excellent tool for school districts to use.

What ENERGY STAR™ Recognitions Are Available?

ENERGY STAR™ offers many opportunities for schools to obtain recognition both locally and nationally. Some of them are outlined here.

The ENERGY STAR™ Label for Buildings: Buildings that receive an energy performance rating of 75 or higher are eligible to apply for the ENERGY STAR™ label for buildings. Facilities that receive this label are among the 25% most energy efficient buildings in the nation.

Building Profiles: Buildings that have received the ENERGY STAR™ Label for Buildings can create a written profile telling about the energy successes realized by that school. This profile will be posted on the ENERGY STAR™ web site and will provide visibility for the school district.

The ENERGY STAR™ Leaders recognition is for organizations that have increased their energy performance rating by at least 10 points on the energy performance rating scale. There is a level of recognition for every 10 point increment of improvement (10, 20, 30, and so on).

Success Stories: ENERGY STAR™ allows school districts to share best practices, lessons learned, and energy performance achievements through success stories. You can develop a success story detailing your energy program achievements and submit it to ENERGY STAR™ for use on their web site.

For more information on these and other ENERGY STAR™ awards and recognitions go to www.energystar.gov.

How Can Energy Data Support the Energy Behavior Management Program?

Once all data is entered into Portfolio Manager for your school campuses and each building has a rating, you can either use the Portfolio Manager report function or export the energy data into an excel spreadsheet and create a variety of reports. These reports can be used to communicate energy performance to all stakeholders and especially to the energy teams working in each building. The more attention the program gets, the more momentum will be created in support of changing District culture.

Top Five Tips for Sharing Energy Data

1. Simple easy to understand report format. A simple and easy to read report format will be most useful in sharing information with a diverse group of people. Not every reader is an engineer or facility expert. Therefore, create a report using terminology everyone can understand.
2. Consistent report creation. Energy team members will expect to see the reports regularly (monthly, bi-monthly, quarterly, and so on). Failure to consistently create and issue these reports will undermine the Energy Behavior Management Program.
3. Distribution to all stakeholders. The energy information will best support the program when it is made available to everyone. In order for this to occur, a distribution system will need to be developed that maximizes the number of readers exposed to the information. Presentation of energy reports to all administrators, the school board, staff, parent groups, and the community will raise awareness, and build support.
4. Transparency. A report format that details the energy results of each school and district campus so that all can see not only how their campus is performing but how everyone else is performing encourages friendly competition. This competition often results in greater effort and more energy savings.
5. Accuracy. The information entered into Portfolio Manager and used to create reports must be accurate and credible. It is best to take data directly from utility bills rather than from in-house generated worksheets.

In managing energy data, the district will need to have an "energy program coordinator" to make sure data is collected, reports are created and distributed, and energy teams get the support they need to do their work. The district can choose to assign these tasks to a staff person or look to a third party to provide these services. However, in order for the Energy Behavior Management Program to be successful a coordinator with time to focus on it must be in place.

What Other Tools Exist for Managing Energy Data?

Portfolio Manager is one of several available tools for managing energy data. It is by far the most widely recognized and as a free service, it is immediately available to all school districts including those with limited funds. There are two major resources I want to discuss here.

1. **Utility Accounting Software**: Both energy accounting and utility accounting software represent a systematic way of recording, analyzing, and reporting energy and other utility costs and usage on a regular basis. Originally, software for this purpose tended to track only energy services (which can be converted to "British Thermal Units") such as electricity, natural gas, propane, oil, etc. As a result, it was called energy accounting software. As software has evolved and "non-energy" utility services such as water, sewer, and garbage were added, the software and the process became known by the broader term "utility accounting". Services provided by utility accounting software include tracking and analyzing utility bill usage and cost, improving the efficiency of processing utility bills for payment, helping locate potential billing errors, and targeting your utility conservation efforts. Utility accounting software programs track all utilities and go beyond what ENERGY STAR™ is intended and designed to do. Many have an ENERGY STAR™ interface so information can be updated in ENERGY STAR™ directly from the utility accounting software and data is only entered one time.

2. **Interval Energy Analysis Software**: Interval energy data is a record of energy consumption with readings made at regular intervals through the day, 24/7. Interval energy data is collected by an interval meter, which, at the end of every interval period (usually 15, 30, and/or 60 minutes), records how much energy was used. Interval energy analysis software accesses this data and converts it into graphs and charts which the school district can use to better manage energy. In some cases, your local electric utility company may offer interval energy analysis software to customers either free or at greatly reduced prices. This is certainly worth checking out. Key questions to ask the local utility include (1) does my school have interval meters and (2) do you offer customers interval energy analysis software?

Exercise #11 – Data Check List

Complete the Data Check List Below To Determine Your Data Starting Point

ENERGY DATA CHECK LIST	ACCOMPLISHED? YES OR NO
Do you have an ENERGY STAR™ Portfolio Manager account set-up?	
Do you have 12 months or more of energy data compiled?	
Have you benchmarked your school buildings for energy use?	
Do you have an energy baseline for your buildings?	
Do you monitor energy usage in school buildings at least monthly?	
Do you use any utility software?	
Do you use any interval data software?	
Do you have any ENERGY STAR™ recognized buildings?	
Do you issue energy reports to stakeholders regularly?	

Energy Benchmarking and Data Management

Key Points to Remember

Benchmarking is the process of comparing the energy usage and performance of your schools to other schools throughout the country.

Baseline and benchmark are similar but distinct activities. A baseline is your building energy performance over a specific period of time and serves as a point of comparison for future reference.

ENERGY STAR™ Portfolio Manager is a free interactive energy management tool that allows you to track and assess energy and water consumption across your entire portfolio of buildings in a secure online environment.

Energy data is an important tool to use in the Energy Behavior Management Program and must be communicated to the entire school community.

Other data tools a school district can use to support the Energy Behavior Management Program include utility accounting software and interval energy analysis software.

NOTES

Chapter Four – The Energy Teams

"Seize this very minute; what you can do, or dream you can, begin it; Boldness has genius, power and magic in it" – *Johann Wolfgang Von Goethe*

The Energy Behavior Management Program model developed in this workbook is the responsibility of the entire school district. Every administrator, every staff member, every campus, every facility person, and every student have responsibilities. An effective structure for the program is to work through energy teams. There are two different types of energy teams at work throughout the program.

1. Energy Advisory Team. The energy advisory team is a group of community leaders, industry professionals, and district staff who are appointed by the superintendent. It is important to have district staff representation include staff from some of the schools. Student representation is also appropriate. The advisory team meets periodically (e.g. quarterly) to review district progress in reaching energy goals and to offer suggestions as to how the program can be improved.
2. Campus Energy Teams. Everybody plays! An energy team is created at every school, administrative center, and support services building. The energy teams become the engines that drive the program. It is their responsibility to design and deliver the Energy Behavior Management Program on their campus.

In this chapter, we will focus our attention on the campus energy teams and discuss membership on the energy team; energy team responsibilities; and activities in which to involve the team.

Energy Team Membership

It is important to structure energy teams correctly from the beginning. At school locations, the principal (or assistant principal) and building support person (facility/maintenance staff) should serve on the team. In addition, teachers, staff, students, and parents representing different grade levels can complete membership. The principal will want to create a process for determining membership which can include an application or nomination process. Ideally, he will want to identify some "energy cheerleaders" early on who will bring their passion to the program and can assist him in finding other members. The size of the team will depend upon how the school chooses to structure and organize the team. If the school wants to have a representative(s) on the team from each grade or allow more student involvement, the team will be larger. There is no right or wrong number of team members in the school.

Administrative and support service buildings are not excluded from creating energy teams. In fact, as visible leaders many will watch to see what they are doing. Over time, their action or lack thereof will be a key indicator of how well the Energy Behavior Management Program performs district wide. Energy teams in these buildings should once again always include administrators and building support staff (facility/maintenance staff). Other staff interested in the cause can complete membership. These teams will generally be smaller in size than teams at the schools.

Exercise #12 – Campus Energy Team Membership

What process will you use to identify energy team membership? Outline your process here. For example, how many members will be on the team? How will they be determined?, and so on...

_____

_____

_____

_____

_____

_____

_____

_____

What is the Role of the Energy Team?

The energy team is responsible for developing an energy plan for their site designed to achieve the annual energy goals and for seeing that the plan is implemented. In some cases, the district will provide an annual energy goal to each site and in others the site will be allowed to set their own. Some of the activities the team will become involved in include managing energy consumption, educating themselves and the school community, and building energy awareness. Let's look at each of these roles in more detail.

Managing Energy Consumption

How much energy does my campus use now? Where is energy being wasted? The first major responsibility the energy team will take on will be to find answers to these questions.

1. **How much energy does my campus use now?** Energy use information for each campus will be tracked and distributed in report format by the district energy coordinator. In addition, the coordinator will have baseline, and energy benchmark ratings from ENERGY STAR™ Portfolio Manager to give to the energy teams. If the district has access to interval data, it would be possible for energy team members to see 24/7 usage data on their computers simply by logging in and using a pass code. Be sure to check with your energy coordinator to see if this is an option for you. Thus, energy data in many forms should be readily available.

2. **Where is energy being wasted?** The energy team will need to conduct an energy audit of their building to determine where energy is wasted. Many energy audit tools are available on the Internet. Samples can be found in Appendix D. Energy audits are a great activity to have students involved in whether they are on the team or not. It is recommended that the energy team do at least one of the following audits. Doing all three would be even better!

    a. Building walk-through with facility/maintenance staff – Walk your campus with facility/maintenance staff who knows the campus well. Use an energy audit checklist and note equipment/structural issues or behavioral practices that are wasteful. For example, if you are walking the campus after school and find lights on in vacated classrooms, computers and monitors left on, and faucets leaking, these are noted as wasteful. The building walk-through will allow team members to observe current energy practices in the school.

b. Plug Load Survey – A significant amount of electricity is used by appliances and devices that are plugged into outlets 24/7. In Arizona, the public utility states that approximately 24% of the electricity used by schools is "plug load." The energy team can walk the building and inventory different items plugged in. In addition, by using an inexpensive device such as a KILL A WATT™ monitor, the actual energy being used by the appliance can be measured along with its cost to the school. The plug load survey will show energy team members how much electricity can be saved by turning off, un-plugging or removing appliances.

c. Waste Audit – How aware are we of the waste we generate? Studies have been done to analyze the contents of the waste stream of schools. Paper makes up the largest component of schools' waste streams. Each student produces about half a pound of waste per school day. The waste audit will show the energy team the quantity of their waste that is recyclable. There are three approaches to the waste audit.

    i. Audit A – have staff, teachers, and students save the garbage from their classroom for one day and then inventory it.

    ii. Audit B – have the energy team conduct a one day audit of classroom and food service waste for one lunch period for the entire school.

    iii. Audit C – have the energy team conduct a visual waste audit of the contents of the school dumpster.

Educating the Energy Team and School Community

The ability of the team to reduce energy consumption on campus depends on how well the team educates the school community about energy, how it is used, and actions that will conserve energy.

After the team has conducted their energy audits, they will be ready to begin to create the energy plan for their campus. A part of that plan should include strategies for educating the community. The possibilities are endless. Do you want to provide a daily or weekly energy tip with daily announcements over the intercom or in newsletters? Do you want to create an energy conservation page on your school or district web site? Can the energy team make presentations at staff meetings or PTA/PTO meetings? What about organizing a special energy assembly or energy fair? These are a few examples of ways the energy team can educate the school community.

Exercise #13 – Educating the School Community

List strategies/actions you will use in educating your school community about the Energy Behavior Management Program? How will you get their buy-in and support?

_____

_____

_____

_____

_____

_____

_____

Building Energy Awareness

Ultimately, Energy Behavior Management Programs succeed because people are constantly reminded to change habits. How do you keep this message in front of everyone on a daily or weekly basis? The energy team will be charged with this responsibility. The energy plan should outline activities to accomplish this. Here are some ideas.

- Institute an Energy Superhero bookmark contest for students. Winning bookmark designs can be made into bookmarks and sold for a school fundraiser.
- Energy awards ceremony. Recognize students and teachers who excel in energy education or in taking energy conservation action.
- Give awards to employees having the best energy conservation ideas.
- Coordinate student involvement as "Energy Patrols" or "Watt Watchers" using energy tickets to write up violations found (lights left on, doors propped open, and so on).
- Place data on light switches indicating dollars wasted by leaving lights on.
- Launch an effort to have everyone in the building turn off personal computers and monitors when not in use, especially overnight and during breaks.
- Implement a reusable water bottle sale to build energy awareness and raise money.
- Sell "green awareness" t shirts using a student design.
- Get involved in Earth Day at the school and create special activities.
- Organize an effort to call companies and ask to be removed from their junk mail list.
- Plant an organic garden.
- Energy fairs.
- Energy awareness day.
- Student and staff energy pledges.
- Green fundraising ideas including lights for learning, cash for recycling, and selling coupons to green businesses.
- Great locker clean out.
- Energy newsletter.
- Energy education programs.
- Top ten list of ways to save energy.
- Energy information web page.
- Workshops for staff, custodians, and students.
- Public recognition for the school.
- Corporate sponsors for the energy initiative.
- Create competitions on campus to see who can perform the most energy conservation tasks during the month and give winners awards.

Writing the Energy Action Plan

Now it's time for the energy team to take all information and data it has gathered and write an energy action plan designed to achieve the energy goals. A sample school energy action plan can be found in Appendix D. Items to address in the plan include:

1. Identify energy team members
2. Identify a campus energy contact person (one of the team members)
3. State the energy goal(s)
4. Create a check list of actions to be taken to achieve each energy goal
5. Create a check list of actions to be taken to educate the school community
6. Create a check list of actions to be taken to build energy awareness
7. Identify any rewards or incentives that will be given for achieving the goal
8. Set timelines and deadlines as appropriate
9. Present the energy plan to the school community and note the date of each presentation (school staff, PTA/PTO, site council, and so on)

Measuring Results

The plan is written and the energy team is busy implementing the various action steps with support from the school community. How will we know if our work is producing the results we want?

Regular energy reports (at least monthly) will be provided to the campus by the energy coordinator showing energy use currently in comparison to energy use in the past. These historical reports will allow the team to monitor progress. Are we using less electricity and water this month than a year ago? Have we reduced our dumpster pickups as a result of recycling activities? Energy reports should be shared with the entire school community.

In addition, the energy team will meet regularly to review the energy action plan and determine which action steps have been accomplished. The team can make regular reports to the school community on progress being made.

Celebrating Success

How exciting will it be when you reach or surpass the goal(s)? As dedicated as the school community is, everyone needs to be recognized for a job well done! What incentives, recognition, and/or rewards will you offer? Will the rewards go to the school, individuals or both? It is important to determine this during the planning process so everyone knows what to expect. You may throw a pizza party to thank the entire school community for their help or perhaps the school district will return a percentage of the money saved to the school.

Success should be celebrated and communicated. Send out a press release touting your savings. Determine how many teaching positions you have saved and let parents know. Inform the school board of your accomplishments at a public meeting. Your success may qualify you for various awards and grants. It will improve the school districts public image with voters and taxpayers! There are many benefits to developing and implementing a quality Energy Behavior Management Program! Take advantage of them all!

Exercise #14 – Celebrating Success

How would you reward the efforts of your school community after they achieve the energy goal(s)? How would you celebrate success?

_____

_____

_____

_____

_____

_____

_____

_____

Exercise #15 – Energy Behavior Management Program Benefits

What benefits do you believe can result from a successful Energy Behavior Management Program?

_____

_____

_____

_____

_____

_____

_____

_____

_____

_____

_____

_____

The Energy Teams

Key Points to Remember

There are two different types of energy teams at work throughout the Energy Behavior Management Program; 1)the energy advisory team appointed by the superintendent and 2)the campus energy teams operating on each school, administrative, and support services campus.

The campus energy teams are the heart and soul of the Energy Behavior Management Program.

The campus energy teams are responsible for developing an energy plan for their site designed to achieve the annual energy goals and seeing that the plan is implemented.

The campus energy teams will conduct one or more energy audits to determine where waste is occurring at their school/building.

The campus energy teams are responsible for writing an energy plan for their school/building designed to achieve the annual energy goal(s).

The campus energy teams are responsible for energy awareness on their campus.

Monthly data reports provided to the campus energy teams by the school district fuel and support their efforts to save energy.

NOTES

Appendix A – Resources

INFORMATIONAL RESOURCES	WEB ADDRESS
Environmental Protection Agency	EPA.gov
ENERGY STAR™	Energystar.gov
Department of Energy	Energy.gov
Energy Smart Schools	Energysmartschools.gov
National Center for Education Statistics	Nces.ed.gov
Alliance to Save Energy	Ase.org
Wilson Educational Services, Inc.	Wilsoned.com
National Energy Education Development Program	NEED.org
United States Green Building Council	USGBC.org
US Green Building Council's Build Green Schools	Buildgreenschools.org
Collaborative for High Performance Schools	CHPS.net
National Clearinghouse for Educational Facilities	Ncef.org
Better Bricks	Betterbricks.com
ENERGY STAR™ Portfolio Manager	https://www.energystar.gov/istar/pmpam/
Energy Plus	Apps1.eere.energy.gov/buildings/energyplus/
ASHRAE Advanced Energy Design Guide for K-12 Schools	Ashrae.org
Planning Guide for Maintaining School Facilities	http://nces.ed.gov/pubs2003/maintenance/
Federal Energy Management Program Operations and Maintenance Best Practices Guide	http://www1.eere.energy.gov/femp/pdfs/omguide_complete.pdf
School Operations and Maintenance Best Practices for Controlling Energy Costs Manual	Asbointl.org
The Collaborative for High Performance Schools Best Practices Guide	CHPS.net

Appendix B – Sample Energy Policy Statements

1. Roger Young, K12 Masters.com – Facilities Excellence Sample Policy

Recognizing our responsibility as Trustees of the _____ School District, we believe that every effort should be made to conserve energy and our natural resources. We also believe that this commitment will be beneficial to our students and taxpayers in prudent financial management and the saving of energy.

The fulfillment of this policy is the joint responsibility of the trustees, administrators, teachers, students, and the support personnel. Cooperation shall be experienced on all levels for the success of this policy.

The district will maintain accurate records of energy consumption and cost of energy on a monthly basis. An energy audit will be conducted annually at each campus and recommendations will be made for updating the energy program. Energy conservation guidelines and procedures will be reviewed and modified as needed by administration. Information will be furnished to the media on the goals and progress of the Energy Behavior Management Program.

2. Christina School District Energy Policy

The Board of Education acknowledges the importance of establishing an official policy governing the Christina School District's use, and conservation of energy. Consequently:

It is Resolved that the official policy, and goal of the Christina School District is to conserve energy where possible and to take a leadership role in developing a realistic energy ethic and awareness of energy needs and costs.

is further resolved that the Superintendent or his or her designee is directed, but not limited to, employing the following methods to achieve this goal:

- Reduce energy consumption in all buildings.
- Implement low cost or no cost operation and maintenance procedures to ensure more efficient equipment operation.
- Assign an energy manager to monitor energy consumption and energy conservation at the district level.

- Establish and communicate energy conservation guidelines.
- Every student and employee shall use his or her best efforts to comply with the district's energy conservation policy and guidelines.
- Building administrators shall judiciously monitor energy use and maintain an efficient energy posture on a daily basis.
- Maintain records of energy consumption and the cost of energy and provide this information to the building leadership.
- Monitor the goals and progress of the energy program and report as appropriate to the board and community at large.

3. **Washington Elementary School District Energy Conservation Policy**

The school board of the Washington Elementary School District is committed to saving energy and contributing to a clean environment and thriving economy for present and future generations by establishing business practices that conserve energy and are environmentally sound. The district will attain these goals by:

- Minimizing its use of electricity, natural gas, water, and other energy resources.
- Promoting an understanding of the importance of environmentally appropriate practices.
- Using best practices in the purchase, use, and disposal of materials.

District staff will implement the following strategies where feasible:

- Reduce the waste of energy, water, paper, food, and other resources by maintaining an Energy Behavior Management Program.
- Use resources efficiently, recycle, and work to reduce the demand for materials and resources like paper, energy, and water.
- Consider environmental impact and societal costs in decision-making.
- Purchase products based on long-term environmental and operating costs.
- Purchase products that are durable, reusable, made of recycled materials, and non-toxic.
- Enlist schools, the community, and business partners to participate in energy conservation strategies and measures.
- Encourage activities that will reduce air pollution such as public transportation, carpooling, and bike riding.
- Promote curriculum on energy conservation, sustainable principles, and the environment.

Appendix C – Sample Energy Standards

Example #1: Christina School District Energy Conservation Guidelines
These guidelines supersede all previous instructions. It is crucial that these energy guidelines be observed in the operation of heating, ventilation, and cooling (HVAC) equipment, and general energy usage. The principal/administrator will be responsible for total energy usage of his/her building. The teacher will be responsible for implementing the guidelines during the time that she/he is present in the classroom. The chief custodians will be responsible for the run times of the HVAC equipment. The energy manager will make available the data reflecting energy consumption to the principal and custodial staff on a monthly basis. The district energy manager will provide support for each building's energy conservation efforts.

A. **Goals for District Energy Program**

1. Conserve energy so that the instructional program and support services can be effectively delivered while conserving energy dollars.
2. Eliminate amounts of energy waste in our buildings while ensuring a comfortable and safe learning environment for all students and staff.
3. Educate every student and employee to contribute to energy efficiency in our district. Every person will be expected to be an "energy saver" as well as an "energy consumer".

B. **Procedures for General Energy Usage**
1. In order to maintain an environment that is conducive to the educational process, the classroom temperature should be in the following range:
   a. Between 75 and 78 degrees during the cooling season (for air conditioned buildings)
   b. Between 68 and 72 degrees during the heating season (in heated areas)
   Note: If temperatures are outside these ranges, report it to the chief custodian.

2. Areas that are not occupied (even if left for a short period of time) will have lighting turned off. After the school day, custodians will use half lighting in the hallways where possible. Custodians will turn on lighting only in areas where they are working or for scheduled facility use.
3. Lights in all gymnasiums, cafeterias, and auditoriums will be off unless the area is being utilized.
4. All outside lights should be turned off during daylight hours.
5. The exhaust fans in the rest rooms will be turned off during periods of time when students are not present.
6. The office staff will turn off copy machines, laminating equipment, and other office machines each night.
7. Teachers will ensure that all classroom PC monitors, local printer, and speakers are turned off during period of time the buildings are not occupied by students. Computer hard drive (CPU units) will be left on around the clock to give the technology department time to install software upgrades, virus protection upgrades, and conduct preventative maintenance to the hard drive (defragmentation). These units should be programmed for the "energy saver" mode using the power management feature.
8. Space heaters use 1000 watts per hour. They are to be **eliminated** from use in all buildings. Flat leg or foot warmers may be substituted and use much less energy (approximately 100 watts per hour). These devices must be turned off at the end of the day.
9. Personal electrical appliances: Refrigerators (compact) are permitted in the classroom with the stipulation that during the winter, spring, and summer breaks the units are unplugged. Coffee pots are permitted in the classroom to brew coffee. Coffee would then be emptied into a thermos type device; and the warmers would be turned off. Microwaves, toaster ovens, and hot plates are not permitted in the classrooms.
10. The chief custodian at each school will be responsible for operating the building in an unoccupied mode at the closing of each school day or scheduled facility use.
11. Any area showing signs of mold should be reported to the chief custodian.

C. **Procedures for Operating Heating Equipment**
1. The thermostat controls shall be set between 68 and 72 degrees during occupied times in the heating season. The district energy manager must approve exceptions in advance.
2. Individual classroom and office doors will be closed when the heating equipment is in operation.
3. In buildings with automatic temperature controls, the start time for the heating equipment should be set as late as possible while allowing time to heat the building to guideline temperature by the beginning of class.
4. In buildings with automatic temperature controls, the temperature will be set at 55 degrees (or appropriate set back temperature based on building history) at the close of the school day or scheduled facility use.
5. The principal will ensure the chief custodian performs end-of-day shutdowns on Monday through Thursday and a weekend shutdown on Friday to make certain that the building systems are set in an energy efficient mode of operation.
6. Domestic hot water systems will be set between 120 F or 140 F for cafeteria service (with dishwasher booster). Ensure all domestic hot water circulating pumps are off during unoccupied times.
7. During spring and fall when there is no threat of freezing, all steam and forced air heating systems will be switched off during unoccupied times. Hot water systems will be switched off using the appropriate loop pumps.
8. If, on extremely cold nights, a 55 degree setback could cause coil freeze ups or not allow the building to heat to a comfortable level by the time students arrive, set the unoccupied temperature setting at 60 degrees.

D. **Procedures for Operating Air Conditioning Equipment**
1. When the temperature is such that cooling is needed at the beginning of the school day, the start time for air conditioning equipment will be set as late as possible while still allowing time to cool the building to guideline temperature settings.
2. Thermostat controls will be set between 75 and 78 degrees when air conditioning is in operation. It is anticipated that by maintaining the 75 to 78 degree thermostat setting, the classroom climate can

be reduced to an even more comfortable level by the use of classroom fans.

3. Refrain from turning lights on unless definitely needed. Remember that lights not only consume electricity, but also give off heat. This places an additional load on the air conditioning equipment and thereby increases the use of electricity necessary to cool the room.

4. The air conditioning equipment will be turned off (or set back based on individual building history) at the approximate time the students leave school. It is anticipated that the temperature of the classroom will be maintained long enough to afford comfort for the period the teacher remains in the classroom after the students have left.

5. Under no circumstances will air conditioning be utilized in classrooms during the summer months unless the classrooms are occupied by students. The district energy manager must approve exceptions.

6. Where cross-ventilation is available during periods of mild weather, shut down air conditioning equipment and adjust the temperature by opening windows and doors.

7. Close individual classroom and office doors when the air conditioning equipment is in operation.

8. In situations when the air conditioning is running in unoccupied areas (ex. floor wax will not dry due to high humidity, indoor air problems, etc...) outside make-up air dampers will be placed in the fully closed position. These situations must have prior approval of the energy manager.

9. Ensure that air conditioning systems operated from automatic temperature controls have outside air dampers closed during unoccupied times.

10. For any 24-hour period the targeted relative humidity should not average greater than 60%.

E. **Procedures for Water Conservation**
1. Ensure that all plumbing (leaks, faucets, flush values, etc.), and/or areas where water is entering the building (i.e. roof leaks, basement water intrusions) or humidity sources (condensation on pipes, sweating walls) are reported, and repaired immediately.

2. All watering should be done between 5:00 am and 10:00 am.

Example#2: Washington Elementary School District

Energy Conservation Guidelines

These guidelines supersede all previous instructions. It is crucial that these energy guidelines be observed in the operation of heating, ventilation, and cooling (HVAC) equipment, and general energy usage. The principal/administrator will be responsible for total energy usage of his/her building. The teacher will be responsible for implementing the guidelines during the time that she/he is present in the classroom and for involving the students in energy conservation. The facility manager will be responsible for the run times of the HVAC equipment. The energy manager will make available the data reflecting energy consumption to the principal and custodial staff on a monthly basis. The district energy manager will provide support for each building's energy conservation efforts.

A. **General Goals for the WESD District Energy Program**
    1. Conserve energy so that the instructional program and support services can be effectively delivered while conserving energy dollars.
    2. Eliminate amounts of energy waste in our buildings while ensuring a comfortable and safe learning environment for all students and staff.
    3. Educate every student and employee to contribute to energy efficiency in our district. Every person will be expected to be an "energy saver" as well as an "energy consumer".

B. **Specific 2008-2009 Energy Goals**
    1. Reduce District electricity usage by 10%.
    2. Reduce District natural gas usage by 10%.
    3. Reduce District water consumption by 10%.
    4. Reduce District waste by 10%.

C. **Procedures for General Energy Usage**
    1. In order to maintain an environment that is conducive to the educational process, the classroom temperature should be in the following range:
        a. Between 74 and 78 degrees during the cooling season (for air conditioned buildings)

b. Between 68 and 72 degrees during the heating season (in heated areas)
    Note: If temperatures are outside these ranges, report it to the facility manager.
2. Areas that are not occupied (even if left for a short period of time) will have lighting turned off. After the school day, custodians will use half lighting in the hallways where possible. Custodians will turn on lighting only in areas where they are working or for scheduled facility use.
3. Lights in all gymnasiums, cafeterias, and auditoriums will be off unless the area is being utilized.
4. All outside lights should be turned off during daylight hours.
5. The exhaust fans in the rest rooms will be turned off during periods of time when students are not present.
6. The office staff will turn off copy machines, laminating equipment, and other office machines each night.
7. Teachers will ensure that all classroom PC monitors, local printer, and speakers are turned off during any period of time the buildings are not occupied by students. Computer hard drive (CPU units) will be left on around the clock to give the technology department time to install software upgrades, virus protection upgrades, and conduct preventive maintenance to the hard drive (de-fragmentation). These units should be programmed for the "energy saver" mode using the power management feature.
8. Space heaters use 1000 watts per hour. They are to be **eliminated** from use in all buildings.
9. Any personal electrical appliances allowed in buildings must be ENERGY STAR™ rated and approved. Refrigerators (compact) are permitted in the classroom with the stipulation that during the winter, spring, and summer breaks the units are unplugged. Coffee pots are permitted in the classroom to brew coffee. Coffee would then be emptied into a thermos type device; and the warmers would be turned off. Microwaves, toaster ovens, and hot plates are not permitted in the classrooms.
10. The facility manager at each school will be responsible for operating the building in an unoccupied mode at the closing of each school day or scheduled facility use.

11. Any area showing signs of mold should be reported to the facility manager.

D. **Procedures for Operating Heating Equipment**
1. The thermostat controls shall be set between 68 and 72 degrees during occupied times in the heating season. The district energy manager must approve exceptions in advance.
2. Individual classroom and office doors will be closed when the heating equipment is in operation.
3. In the buildings with automatic temperature controls, the start time for the heating equipment should be set as late as possible while allowing time to heat the building to guideline temperature by the beginning of class.
4. In buildings with automatic temperature controls, the temperature will be set at 55 degrees (or appropriate set back temperature based on building history) at the close of the school day or scheduled facility use.
5. The principal will ensure that the facility manager performs end-of-day shutdowns on Monday through Thursday and a weekend shutdown on Friday to make certain that the building systems are set in an energy efficient mode of operation.
6. Domestic hot water systems will be set between 120 F or 140 F for cafeteria service (with dishwasher booster). Ensure all domestic hot water circulating pumps are off during unoccupied times.
7. During spring and fall when there is no threat of freezing, all steam and forced air heating systems will be switched off during unoccupied times. Hot water systems will be switched off using the appropriate loop pumps.
8. If, on extremely cold nights, a 55 degree setback could cause coil freeze ups or not allow the building to heat to a comfortable level by the time students arrive, set the unoccupied temperature setting at 60 degrees.

E. **Procedures for Operating Air Conditioning Equipment**
1. When the temperature is such that cooling is needed at the beginning of the school day, the start time for air conditioning equipment will be set as late as possible while still allowing time to cool the building to guideline temperature settings.

2. Thermostat controls will be set between 74 and 78 degrees when air conditioning is in operation. It is anticipated that by maintaining the 74 to 78 degree thermostat setting, the classroom climate can be reduced to an even more comfortable level by the use of classroom fans.
3. Refrain from turning lights on unless definitely needed. Remember that lights not only consume electricity, but also give off heat. This places an additional load on the air conditioning equipment and thereby increases the use of electricity necessary to cool the room.
4. The air conditioning equipment will be turned off (or set back based on individual building history) at the approximate time the students leave school. It is anticipated that the temperature of the classroom will be maintained long enough to afford comfort for the period the teacher remains in the classroom after the students have left.
5. Under no circumstances will air conditioning be utilized in classrooms during the summer months unless the classrooms are occupied by students. The district energy manager must approve exceptions.
6. Where cross-ventilation is available during periods of mild weather, shut down air conditioning equipment and adjust the temperature by opening windows and doors.
7. Close individual classroom and office doors when the air conditioning equipment is in operation.
8. In situations when the air conditioning is running in unoccupied areas (ex. floor wax will not dry due to high humidity, indoor air problems, etc...) outside make-up air dampers will be placed in the fully closed position. These situations must have prior approval of the energy manager.
9. Ensure that air conditioning systems operated from automatic temperature controls have outside air dampers closed during unoccupied times.
10. For any 24-hour period the targeted relative humidity should not average greater than 60%.

F. **Procedures for Water Conservation**
  1. Ensure that all plumbing (leaks, faucets, flush values, etc.), and/or areas where water is entering the building (i.e. roof leaks, basement water intrusions) or humidity sources (condensation on pipes, sweating walls) are reported and repaired immediately.
  2. All watering should be done between 1:00 am and 5:00 am.

G. **Procedures for Waste Management**
  1. The WESD will establish a district recycling program. Each school campus will have recycling dumpsters for paper.
  2. Recycling dumpsters will be placed in a location on the school campus approved by the energy manager.
  3. Each school will create a system for assuring that disposed of paper gets from the classroom/office areas to the paper recycling container.
  4. Other recycling procedures will be announced as the program expands.

Appendix D — Energy Team Materials

Building Walk Through Survey Instructions

Objective: Document efficient energy behaviors and wasted energy behaviors in the rooms you audit; document equipment and system defects that could waste energy.

Participants: Energy Team and Facility/Maintenance Staff.

Using the survey document, enter a room and fill in the date and time at the top of the form. Fill in the columns from left to right starting with the room number. Moving from column to column use a "check mark" to record positive energy behaviors and an "x" to indicate negative energy behaviors. For example, if the room is empty and lights or equipment is left on put an "x" in the box under lighting and the related items. If the room is empty and lights or equipment are turned off, put a "check mark" in the box under lighting and related items.

Appliances in a classroom can be either a positive or a negative depending upon the policy of the school district. Some districts do not allow personal appliances in the classroom. If this is the case at your school and you find an appliance in a classroom you would mark an "x" in the box. If your school district allows personal appliances and you find a coffeemaker in an empty classroom but it is turned off and unplugged, you would put a "check mark" in the column. You will have to use some discretion in completing the survey.

Windows and doors should be closed at all times. Put a "check" if they are closed or an "x" if they are open. If your school has heating, ventilation, and cooling units inside the classroom make certain they are clear from any obstruction. If there is an obstruction such as books, boxes, anything sitting on or in front of the unit, place an "x" in the HVAC column of the form. Bring along a note pad for writing down details and specifics that cannot be recorded in the survey form.

BUILDING WALK THROUGH SURVEY

Date:		Time:									
Classroom	Room #	Lights	Computer Monitors	Printers	Personal Appliances	HVAC Units	Doors Closed	Windows Closed	Other	Total √	Total X
Non-Classroom	Room #	Lights	Computer Monitors	Printers	Personal Appliances	HVAC Units	Doors Closed	Windows Closed	Other	Total √	Total X

Key Codes:

√ = on/in use & ok or no energy in use

X = on with no people

Time Codes:

BS = Before School

LR = Lunch/Recess

AS = After Schools

SURVEY TAKEN FROM "Blueprint for School Energy Teams"
THE KENTUCKY NEED PROJECT – WWW.NEED.ORG

PLUG LOAD WORKSHEET

INSTRUCTIONS: Inventory equipment in a room. You can inventory an entire building or take one or two classrooms; one or two non-classroom spaces; one or two office spaces to establish a baseline and multiple your findings by the total number of that type of space in the building. This will give you a good estimate of a buildings plug load.

1000 watts = 1 kWh (kilowatt hour)

Average Electricity Cost per kWh = Q. Check with your local utility company to determine you kWh rate. The national average rate is $0.081 per kWh.

Average CO2 emitted per kWh = 0.77 lbs.

	A	B	C	D	E	F	G	H	I	J
				(A x B x 20 Days)	(C x D/1000)	# Mos. in Use	(E x F)	(G/A x Q)	(G x Q)	(G x 0.77)
Equipment	Quantity in Use	Typical Use, Hrs./Day	Average Running Wattage	Total Running Hrs./Mo.	Monthly kWh	Months Per Year	Yearly kWh	Annual Cost Each	Total Annual Cost	Annual CO2 Emissions (lbs.)
EXAMPLE	2	7	125	280	35	9	315	$12.76	$25.52	242.55
TOTAL										

SURVEY TAKEN FROM "Blueprint for School Energy Teams"
THE KENTUCKY NEED PROJECT – WWW.NEED.ORG

SCHOOL WASTE AUDIT

Type of Material	Estimated Percentages (Visually estimate or weigh the materials)	Location Found		Check the box below to indicate what can be done with the materials found during the waste audit.					
				Compost	Reduce	Reuse	Recycle	Donate or Exchange	Dumpster
Mixed Paper									
Cardboard									
Plastic Bottles #1 (PETE) #2 (HDPE)									
Glass Bottles, and Jars									
Aluminum Cans									
Newspaper									
Food Waste									
Polystyrene #6									
Other Plastics #3, #4, #4, #7									
Misc. Items Textiles, Electronics									
Other Waste									

AUDIT FORM TAKEN FROM WWW.RECYCLEWORKS.ORG

SAMPLE School District

_____School

Energy Plan

July 2010

Created By Energy Team Members:

Date Approved by Site Council:

Date Presented to Staff:

_____ School supports the school board and Superintendent of the SAMPLE School District and is committed to saving energy and contributing to a clean environment and thriving economy for present and future generations. In support of the District energy goals, _____ School will establish business practices that conserve energy and are environmentally sound.

Saving energy is all about educating each other and changing habits. With this understanding, it is our intention to involve our entire school community in our efforts: staff, students, parents, volunteers, and the neighborhood. Some of the activities we plan to organize are:

School Energy Awareness Checklist

☐ Write a Building Energy Plan by {insert date}.

☐ Host a "Save the Earth Day."

☐ Integrate energy conservation into the curriculum.

☐ Monitor energy usage monthly and share results with everyone.

☐ Have students, staff, parents, and community take the Energy Pledge.

☐ Create a Building Energy Rewards Program.

☐ Put up signs and posters and hand out literature.

☐ Have energy as a theme for the science fair.

☐ Allow students to be Energy Police.

☐ Educate through the school newsletter.

Other Positive Actions (List On Attached Page)

Our first goal is to reduce our consumption of electricity by a minimum of 10% during the 2010-2011 school year. In order to accomplish this, we plan to take the following positive actions:

Electricity Conservation Checklist:

☐ Turn out the lights when leaving an area.

☐ Keep thermostats between 74-78 when cooling.

☐ Keep thermostats between 68-72 when heating.

☐ Remove small appliances from classrooms.

☐ Use only ENERGY STAR™ appliances.

☐ Turn off all equipment daily. (computers, printers, etc.)

☐ Close doors/windows tightly if cooling or heating.

☐ Use natural light and keep lights off.

Other Positive Actions (List on Attached Page)

In addition, we are committed to conserving water. We pledge to take the following actions:

Water Conservation Checklist:
☐ Turn off faucets.
☐ Report toilet and faucet leaks immediately.
☐ Water outside spaces only from 7 p.m. - 6 a.m.
☐ Plant vegetation requiring less watering.
☐ Water outside spaces only as needed.
☐ Check sprinklers and report leaks immediately.
Other Positive Actions (List on Attached Page)

We are committed to recycling and using the motto "reduce, reuse, recycle" at our school. We will do the following:

<u>Recycling Checklist:</u>

☐ Collect paper and put it into the recycling dumpster.

☐ Collect cardboard for recycling.

☐ Involve students in recycling efforts.

☐ Stack trays in the cafeteria after eating lunch.

Other Positive Actions (List on Attached Page)

The energy contact person for our building will be

       Name:

       Phone Number:

       E-mail Address:

NOTES

NOTES

NOTES

About the Author

Sue Pierce is the principal of Pierce and Associates Company, Inc., a professional service company that offers facility and energy planning and consulting services to K-12 schools and other public entities. Ms. Pierce has worked as a consultant to local government and school districts for 22 years. Serving as executive director of a public policy research organization from 1988 – 1994, she had the opportunity to use both her finance and public policy skill sets to effect significant change in Iowa.

In 1994, Ms. Pierce resigned as executive director to start Pierce and Associates. She has been engaged by several school districts, cities, and counties to design and implement broad-based facility planning efforts, to run referendums, and create high performance facilities focused on energy conservation and an improved work and learning environment. Her extensive work with school districts includes providing a variety of planning services in the areas of facilities, energy, green initiatives, and finance. Ms. Pierce is frequently a speaker on energy and facility issues at school conventions and trainings, a presenter on energy topics at national webinars including Facility Masters, School Dude and Energy Smart Schools Department of Energy webinars.

Ms. Pierce has been an active community leader serving on various local and state boards including the Chamber of Commerce, United Way, Goodwill Industries, the Susan B Komen Breast Cancer Foundation, and USGBC LEED for Schools Committee. She was chosen by her peers to receive the "Woman of Excellence" Award in the category of "women pursuing truth", and has earned placement in America's directory of "Who's Who Among American Professional Women." Susan is married to Dean Pierce and currently resides in Cave Creek, Arizona. You can contact Sue at sue@energyplanning.org.

www.ingramcontent.com/pod-product-compliance
Lightning Source LLC
La Vergne TN
LVHW061228060426
835509LV00012B/1466